Oral Patterns of Performance

Story and Song

Barre Toelken

Oral Patterns of Performance: Story and Song comprises chapter 4 from
The Anguish of Snails: Native American Folklore in the West, by Barre
Toelken. © 2003 by University Press of Colorado

Published by Utah State University Press
An imprint of University Press of Colorado
5589 Arapahoe Avenue, Suite 206C
Boulder, Colorado 80303

The University Press of Colorado is a proud member of The Association of
American University Presses.

The University Press of Colorado is a cooperative publishing enterprise sup-
ported, in part, by Adams State University, Colorado State University, Fort
Lewis College, Metropolitan State University of Denver, Regis University,
University of Colorado, University of Northern Colorado, Utah State
University, and Western State Colorado University.

Library of Congress Cataloging-in-Publication Data for the book *The Anguish of
Snails Native American Folklore in the West*

Toelken, Barre.
The anguish of snails : Native American folklore in the West / Barre Toelken.
p. cm. — (Folklife of the West ; v. 2)
Includes bibliographical references and index.
ISBN 0-87421-556-0 (pbk. : alk. paper) — ISBN 0-87421-555-2 (hardback:
alk. paper)
1. Indians of North America—West (U.S.)—Folklore. 2. Folklore—
Performance—West (U.S.) 3. Folklore—West (U.S.)—Classification. 4. Oral
tradition—West (U.S.) I. Title. II. Series.
E78.W5T642003
398'.089'97078—dc21

                    2003006172

Current Arguments in Folklore edition, 2014
ISBN 978-0-87421-967-8 (paper)
ISBN 978-0-87421-953-1 (ebook)
DOI: 10.7330/9780874219531.c001

Contents

Oral Patterns of Performance: Story and Song

Everything is made possible through stories.

> —Hugh Yellowman, Navajo,
> explaining why stories are told

I've been poor most of my life; I've known only one song.

> —Little Wagon, Navajo,
> on the importance of songs

Eʀʟʏ ɪɴ ᴛʜᴇ Nᴀᴠᴀᴊᴏ ᴄʀᴇᴀᴛɪᴏɴ sᴛᴏʀʏ, Fɪʀsᴛ Mᴀɴ and First Woman (who are depicted as gendered holy beings made up of colored light), hear a strange noise on a nearby mountain shrouded by clouds. Apprehensive about what this unknown noise may signify, but feeling a need to investigate, First Man rejects First Woman's advice to avoid the dangers, saying:

> *Do not be afraid . . .*
> *Nothing will go wrong. For I will surround myself with song.*
> *I will sing as I make my way to the mountain.*
> *I will sing while I am on the mountain.*
> *And I will sing as I return.*
> *I will surround myself with song.*
> *You may be sure that the words of my song will protect me.*[1]

What First Man finds on the mountain is a baby girl, crying; it is Changing Woman, the first real personage in Navajo mythic history, and the closest to a full deity of all the sacred people (*yei*) in the Navajo pantheon. He brings her back to First Woman, and the two, totally clueless about what to do with a baby, set about ritualizing her life and physical development by creating proper words and stories.

Much of the Beautyway story and ceremony focuses on the discovery and maturation of Changing Woman, and today, whenever a hogan is blessed, or a wedding is performed, or a young woman celebrates her first menstruation, songs from this extensive ceremony are sung, the words vividly dramatizing for contemporary people their identity with the sacred past. For Navajos, actually uttering words creates the reality of their world: Spoken or sung language is a creative act; hence, people avoid speaking of things they don't want to see appear in the world around them. One of the most terrible things to say out loud (if a Navajo carpenter pounds his thumb with a hammer, for instance) is *shash*, "bear," for—uttered in passion—the word may really summon a bear, and bears are ritually (and factually) difficult to deal with.

Spoken words, especially when enhanced or intensified by repetition, ritual structures, and musical phrases, are the principal means Navajos use to create a sense of order and harmony in the world they inhabit. The medicines administered to a patient in any Navajo healing ceremony are a response to the symptoms being treated, but healing in any deeper sense comes through the power of the words in the ritual. Along with doing sand paintings (which are symmetrical, cyclic, oriented to the universe, and usually four sided), placing the ritual inside a hogan (which is round, oriented to the east, and represents the womb of Changing Woman), and using four-way repetition in the songs (which represents the four directions), Navajo curing ceremonies have the same patterns and assumptions we have been discussing. Most of these rituals are not secret and are not conducted by mysterious shamans but by *hataaii*, literally "singers," who may be either male or female (hence the uselessness of the stereotypical English term "medicine man") and spend about fifteen to twenty years learning the songs, sand paintings, stories, and medications for one ceremony or "Way." Most of these singers know several Ways, which are healing rituals envisioned as moving along a trail; obviously, even mastering one is an intellectual achievement of some distinction.

By contrast, a *shaman* (the term is based on a Siberian Tungus word, so the second syllable has nothing to do with gender) is defined as a person who has gained control over the processes of life and death—usually by having died and come back to life. Shamans are most active in cultures which depend on a lively interaction between the living and the dead—hunting cultures are the most prominent examples—where the death of animal relatives is explained and mediated, and breaches with the animal world healed, by the magical ability of the shaman to visit the world of dead animals. Such a person would be called a witch by the Navajos and other southwestern tribes, mostly agriculturalists, whose way of viewing reality entails the verbal encouragement of health and fertility for plants and people alike.

Much has been written about these ceremonies, and since our object is to deal with expressions readily available to outsiders, I want only to call special attention to the concept of the creative power in spoken words. When I was a patient in a Beautyway ceremony a few years ago (urged on me by my adoptive Navajo family to promote stability in my life), we reached the part of the story where the Hero Twins, sons of Changing Woman (fathered by the Sun and some drops of water since there were no men yet), are on their way to visit their father, the Sun, who is protected by powerful warriors whose job it is to fight off anyone who approaches. Not only was the story being told—in part through ritual songs—but we were to think of ourselves as actually being there, floating up to the Sun on the same feather that was transporting the Hero Twins, empowered by the words uttered by the singer. As we got closer to the Sun and the battle became fiercer, my Navajo family members began shouting words of encouragement like "Don't give up!" "We're almost there!" "Protect us with your spear!" What I had been doing for an hour during the ceremony was holding over my head a foot-long, chipped stone spearhead, which was in fact getting heavier every second. The singer, Jimmie Descheeny, had also tied a row of stone arrowheads around my head, and I began to realize that these armaments were my means to reach the Sun and assure the safety of those traveling with me; I, the sick one, provided the only protection. After our success, which was celebrated with several fourfold song stanzas, the story described us returning to earth on a lightning bolt. Imaginary, you may say. Sure, in the same way a gripping play or film is imaginary: If it's done right, it becomes a very vivid experience.

Not all tribes believe that spoken language is creative in the same way the Navajos do, but every tribe I know believes that songs and stories are dramatic enactments of reality which go far beyond mere entertainment. A good story is like an effective ritual: It puts you there, makes you experience or reexperience something. And that something is an otherwise-abstract but real idea from your culture, made concrete and experiential through the imagination and knowledge which you bring to the story performance, enhanced by the power of the performer.

Indeed, narrative structure is so central to human thinking that some scientists believe that *story* is the engram of our species.[2] In the same vein, John D. Niles, a scholar of oral literature, has argued that we should be called *Homo narrans* (storytelling man). In the following songs and stories, then, let's take story structure and song nuance seriously and ask, "What does this song or story dramatize or embody?" (not "What does it describe?" or "What does it explain?"). Many Native stories end with a formula like "and that's how the bear got a short tail," leading listeners to assume that such tales are primitive (and childish) ways of accounting for the features of the natural world. But when you ask the storytellers, they don't see the story as an explanation of anything but rather, an enactment of something: A bear is dramatized as lazy, or uncaring, or selfish, or careless; because he fails to act appropriately, he gets his tail caught in the ice, and, persisting in being selfish or egotistical (instead of calling for help), he tears himself loose and leaves his tail stuck there.

When we hear the story, we're reminded of how personally damaging and painful it is—even for someone who is large and powerful—to be lazy, uncaring, selfish, or careless. When we see a bear in the world around us, we notice the short tail and recall the story and our cultural obligations. Once again—this time through a story—the animal becomes (and through oral tradition remains) our mentor. Interpreting the story as a serious explanation of bear physiology is equivalent to seeing "The Three Little Pigs" as a serious report on porcine behavior.

A good example of the dramatic patterning of cultural abstracts through narrative occurs in a story performed by a Lummi (Northwest coast) woman for Jan H. Brunvand, Joseph Campbell, and me while we were speaking at a symposium at Western Washington State University in the late 1960s. None of us had brought a tape recorder, so the following is not verbatim but reconstituted from my notes, not by any means an ideal situation but acceptable because the story itself—even partially recaptured—is quite powerful. The woman spoke in English but said she had grown up hearing the story in Lummi. Because it was a story reflecting her tribe's traditions and not her own ideas, she said we could use it—for it was not secret—as long as we didn't associate her name with it. She didn't give it a title, but I identify it in my mind as "The Five Lummi Sisters." Here is the written version; the separate paragraphs indicate segments of the story, not her performance dynamics.

Five sisters went out to get huckleberries; each one carried two baskets.

When they got out there where the huckleberries grew, they saw that the bushes were just covered with big huckleberries. There were way more than they could ever pick, so they knew they'd get all they wanted.

The oldest sister said, "Look at all these huckleberries! We can fill our baskets easily." So they held their baskets under the bushes and shook the berries in. Right away they all had their baskets full, so they sat down in the shade to rest.

The oldest sister said, "Look; there are plenty of berries. It's a nice warm day, and we could just eat these berries and fill our baskets again before we go home." So they ate all the berries they had picked, and then they turned the baskets over and hit them against their legs like this [slapping her hands a few times against her thighs] to knock all the leaves and stems out. And so they went back to the bushes and started picking again. Again their baskets filled right up with no trouble at all.

The second sister said, "Those berries were really good, and look how many more there are. If we don't eat them, the birds will just get them. Why don't we eat these and then get some more before we go home?" So they sat down again and ate all the berries they had picked. Then they beat their baskets against their legs again like this [slapping her thighs a few times] to knock all the leaves and stems out. It took them a little longer to get rid of all those leaves. Then they went back to the bushes and picked some more. Just knocked them off the bushes into their baskets, and they got full baskets again right away.

The third sister said, "Look how many berries are still there! The birds will get them if we don't. Let's eat these we've picked and then fill our baskets again before going home." So they sat down again and ate all the berries. After they rested a while, they got up and slapped the baskets against their legs like this [slaps her thighs a few times] to get the leaves and stems out, and it took even longer this time. Finally, they went back to the bushes and began pushing the berries into their baskets, and their baskets got full right away.

The fourth sister said, "Those berries were so good! I'd like to eat some more. There are still plenty of berries here. Let's sit down and rest and eat these. We can still fill up our baskets again before going home." So they sat down and ate the berries, and afterward they knocked the baskets against their legs again like this [slaps her thighs several times] to get rid of the stems and leaves and little bugs. And it took a long time to clean out the baskets. They went back to the bushes and began picking again. Actually, they didn't even have to pick: The berries just fell off, and right away they had all their baskets full again.

The youngest sister said, "Those berries were warm and sweet, and I'd like to eat some more before we go home. There are still plenty left for us and for the birds." So they sat down again and ate everything they had picked. They got up. They started knocking the baskets against their legs [slaps her thighs continuously through the rest of this sentence], but they couldn't stop, and their arms went higher and higher, and they kept hitting the baskets against their legs, and they couldn't stop until finally, they lifted off the ground, flapping their arms faster and faster, and they flew away.

They became the birds. That's where birds came from. That's all.

Now, if we read that last line as the meaning of the story, we have a conceptual problem because how can a story where the birds already exist and the characters refer to them explain the origin of birds? So let's start elsewhere: What's dramatized by this story and how? At the same time, it's appropriate to ask, "What does the Lummi audience know that I don't? What do they bring to this dramatic experience that makes the narrative mean something for them?"

What is clear is that between the simple opening and closing sentences is a sequence of five events—all practically the same. Five is the standard dramatic number in Pacific Northwest narratives, just as three is the standard Euro-American number, and four is the most common number in the Southwest. But this is more important than just observing that different cultures prefer different numbers: These are methods of thinking about the relationship among the narrative parts. The one-two-three lineal sequence we are so familiar with in Euro-American jokes, tales, ballads, and even personal anecdotes usually comes to some point on count three (the third little pig is the one who keeps the wolf from the door; the third try is the charm). The Southwest use of four, since it refers to the main directions, almost always suggests surroundment, encirclement, focus; in stories structured in fours, there is no punch line or result, for the device is not envisioned as lineal. Rather, the listeners know that if something is repeated four times, the event is important and may even have ritual significance.

The Northwest five may be patterned after the fingers of the hand, for in many cases (as in the beginning of "The Sun's Myth," discussed next), it suggests completeness, wholeness. Within a story, the device is not used unless the idea repeated five times is important. In a way, it is a kind of oral italics, a means of intensifying. So, while a non-Northwest person may see the repetitions in "The Five Lummi Sisters" as needless redundancy, the Northwest Native understands they are a sign that the action of eating berries and dumping baskets has considerable consequence.

Why would eating and dumping be so important though? Part of the answer can be inferred already by anyone who has eaten a great quantity of berries; eating is fun, but getting rid of the byproducts can be problematic. But the story offers us more than gratuitous advice about diarrhea. In virtually every tribe, food gathered and hunted away from the village should not be consumed until it's brought back to be shared with family and other villagers. Eating gathered food by yourself, away in the woods, is a form of gluttony and viewed by most tribes—unless it's a case of raw survival—as antisocial. When the *oldest* sister, who should be the most knowledgeable in the customs and values of her people, makes the first move to break the code, it makes it easier for the younger ones to follow. Incrementally, as the human social order breaks down, the girls go out of control and become birds. Why birds? Observe them, and you'll notice that they eat berries, dump the residue, and spend most of their time bringing food back to their nests for their families. For their inattention to social values, the girls become living icons of the social principle of sharing; the birds remind us of the idea as they fly by—the beating of their wings sounds like baskets against girls' thighs.

Another pattern in Native narrative can be called *reciprocative structure*. Some years ago, John Bierhorst suggested that many Native American myths are structured in two parts, one reflecting, expanding, or reciprocating the other.[3] In another story, also from the Pacific Northwest, the device achieves great power. "The Sun's Myth" was collected in 1891 by Franz Boas, who took it down phonetically from the dictation of Charles Cultee, one of the last three speakers of the Kathlamet Chinook language. This language is no longer spoken (in fact, the last speaker died only a few years after Boas collected the story), and people who would have understood all the nuances of the story are long gone. Thus, while we have no hope of knowing fully what this myth dramatized, we can extrapolate from hints in the story, as well as customs and traditions of nearby related tribes, and reach a provisional understanding.

For one thing, we know that the Chinooks usually named their myths after the most important character in the narrative, not necessarily the one who appears most often. Thus, the focus in this myth is the Sun, and she is female. As an older female, she naturally provides nourishment and ritual propriety for her family. The baseline is ancient, continual, and traditional nurturance by a female head of family (and since she is the Sun, we may suppose this family includes us).

With that as a lead, we can look at the other females in the narrative: What roles do they play? The wife of the chief who wants to visit the Sun tries to dissuade him, implying that he's foolish to think he can go there. This is a subtle form of Native persuasion; since Native behavior is almost never prescriptive, mentors delicately suggest advice, but an individual's decision is his or her own responsibility. By rejecting or ignoring his wife's suggestion, the chief is taking personal responsibility for a rash decision. Like a traditional wife, she does not argue but helps him prepare. Later in the story, he encounters another younger, unmarried woman, and she, too, tries to give him guidance but to no avail.

All this is important for us to track because otherwise we might misread the story, which at first sounds like a Western "hero myth," in which a daring man goes into the world to bring back some kind of prize for his people. Instead, we must see this story as a man intruding his own egotistical agenda into a traditional way of life. The result? Not a blessing for his people but destruction.

The story, presented here in summarized segments, follows Dell Hymes's brilliant translation, which has been published several times with ever-finer tuning since its first appearance in the *Journal of American Folklore* in 1976.[4] Hymes presents the narrative as a two-act play with distinct scenes. Remembering Bierhorst's suggestion that these two acts may be restatements or reflections of each other, let's look at "The Sun's Myth," incorporating everything we now know (or think we know) about the cultural constructions of Northwest narrative. Granted, we are unable to deal with the actual language and its nuances, or the performance styles of traditional Kathlamet narrators, for all of that has been lost. But through Hymes's painstaking reconstruction of the original phonetic text in comparison with nearby dialects still in use, we have a pretty accurate articulation of the story line, and that's something.

The story opens with a couple of lines that seem to function like the first lines of "The Five Lummi Sisters": It describes the normal setting, in and from which the action unfolds:

> *They live there, those people of a town.*
> *Five the towns of his relatives, that chief.*

It is not clear whether he is chief of all five villages or one village connected with four others by family ties. But in any case, there's our Northwest number *five*, which tells us that this chief is part of a considerable, complete family cluster. Keep in mind that in most tribes it is the family, not the individual, which constitutes the basic social unit; also remember that the chief of most Northwest coastal groups was an influential person who did not simply order other people around (as they are depicted in our movies: "Mmm! We go to war!")

but presided over social events and rituals like hunting and fishing expeditions (which provided nurture for everybody) and arranged festive occasions when people gave goods away to others in their communities. Sometimes called "potlatches" (more commonly, "giveaways" today), these events were chances for people to demonstrate their wealth and power by giving everything away. The Northwest tribes were surrounded by food: fish and mammals in the rivers and ocean; deer, elk, and moose in the nearby forests. They apparently spent a lot less time making their living than we do in our culture, and the bulk of their time went into producing gorgeous artistic items, ranging from totem poles and other carvings, to baskets and boxes, to cured hides and woven blankets. They loved material wealth, but in any tribal situation, one person accumulating extreme wealth can cause envy, so one of their favorite things to do with wealth was redistribute it to the entire community on ritual occasions such as maturation ceremonies, weddings, funerals, the dedication of a new house, the birth of a child, or virtually any important moment. The chief's job would have given him a central role in the enactment of these continual orgies of redistribution.

Our chief, in spite of these cultural expectations, wants to go on a personal journey.

He goes outside every morning and stares at the sun as it partially appears through the heavy clouds of the south Washington coast (where the Columbia flows into the Pacific). He asks his wife what she would think if he went to visit the Sun. She says, incredulously, "You think it is near?" and asks if he really wants to go there. Not accepting her hint that he's being unrealistic, he keeps going out every morning and finally tells his wife to make him ten pairs of moccasins (five times two pairs) and ten leggings. She complies without further comment (as if to say, "Okay, then; it's your decision").

He sets out in the morning, and over a long journey eventually wears out all of his moccasins and leggings, arriving at last at a large house (normally the indication of a family with an important place in the community). Inside is a young girl, alone, surrounded by culturally important items hanging on the walls in magnificent abundance. The storyteller catalogues these riches for the next fifty-eight lines, detailing the arrows, armor, axes, clubs, regalia ("men's property") on one wall, and the blankets, skins, and dentalia beads (presumably "women's property"`) on the other. The chief asks thirteen times who owns these items, and in every case he is told the same thing: They belong to the girl and her grandmother, the girl says, and they are being saved for "my maturity," that is, for the giveaway/potlatch that will be held when she celebrates her first menstruation—an event which will socially and ritually signal the fact that she is marriageable. The chief's response? "I will take her." He moves in with the girl and her grandmother (who, we find out, is the Sun). He "takes" the young girl and lives there for a long time, watching the older woman come back every evening loaded with more blankets, arrows, and armor.

Let's stop for a moment to reflect on the first part of this drama: A chief who would normally be in the center of a culture, helping distribute goods on special occasions and encouraging proper behavior, has moved into someone else's house without invitation and appropriated goods which should have been distributed to others at a proper time, and has taken a prepubescent young girl who is not yet eligible to be married. What an irony: Not just anybody but someone who should be the epitome of tribal propriety has now become, through his own selfishness and aggressive behavior, the icon of culturally destructive values. We should not be surprised if the second half of the drama expands on this idea by acting it out in bloody detail.

Part II begins with the chief sleeping, not getting up. The young girl and her grandmother recognize this as a sign of what we would call depression and conclude that he is homesick. The old lady, the Sun, asks him what he would like to take with him when he goes home: some buffalo skins? some mountain-goat blankets? She shows him virtually everything, but he refuses it all. He wants only one bright thing he has seen among her belongings, and he insists on taking it with him. The old woman refuses him several times, then finally gives in the same way his wife and the young girl have already done in response to his insistence—not, we must conclude, because they are weak but because it's a way of focusing our attention on the chief's willfulness, the fruits of which are about to be acted out with a vengeance: His moral defect is being dramatized against the backdrop of normal, nurturing, female deportment. Reluctantly, and with obvious misgivings, the old lady hangs the shining object on him (we are never told exactly what it is, but a later passage suggests it is a kind of blanket), gives him a stone ax, and after reminding him, "It is you who choose," sends him on his way home.

In contrast to the tedious outward journey, the homeward move is almost instantaneous. As he arrives near an uncle's town, the shining object begins to throb and speak: "We two shall strike your town." Losing his reason and using his stone ax, he crushes the entire town and everyone in it, covering himself with blood. As he recovers, he begins to blame the shining object ("Why was I made to love this?") and tries unsuccessfully to get rid of it. He tries shaking it

off, but it seems attached to his flesh. As he approaches each
of his uncles' villages, the same thing happens: He goes into
a frenzy, crushes the whole village and its inhabitants, and
then, still blaming the object and not his own selfishness,
attempts to get rid of both the shining blanket and the stone
ax, but "always those fingers of his would cramp." He cannot
rid himself of the tools of destruction. Now he approaches his
own town (where his wife and immediate family live), and he
destroys it as well until "the dead fill the ground." Weeping,
he looks back and sees the old woman, the Sun, standing
nearby. In a lyrically quiet passage (after the frantic activity of
destruction), she reminds him that he is responsible for what
has happened.

In Hymes's carefully worded epilogue, the story ends like
this:

He looked back	*VI(A)*
Now she is standing near him, that old woman	*300*
"You,"	
She told him,	
"You.	
In vain I try to love you,	
in vain I try to love your relatives.	*305*
Why do you weep?	
It is you who choose;	
now you carried that blanket of mine."	
Now she took it,	*(B)*
she lifted off what he had taken;	*310*
now she left him,	
she went home.	
He stayed there;	*(C)*
he went a little distance;	
there he built a house,	*315*
a small house.	

It is impossible to overlook the contrast between the long journey at the beginning of Part I and the quick return at the beginning of Part II. Similarly, it's hard to miss the contrast between the large, opulent house at the end of Part I and the small empty house at the end of Part II. If we assume the two parts are reciprocal in dramatizing an idea, what is that idea? One set of possibilities is this: A compulsive, energetic move away from your obligations just to satisfy a selfish whim is the fastest way to do something destructive to your culture. Taking over a large house full of objects you have no rightful claim to is the equivalent of impoverishing yourself. And if we compare the two most heavily descriptive and detailed segments of the story—the catalog of gorgeous stuff the chief first admires and then takes in Part I, and the village-by-village destruction of his own people in Part II—we can see the dramatization of the concept that the selfish, unritualized taking of culturally dedicated goods in violation of the culture's values (especially by someone who should know better, as implied by the women in this story) literally destroys your culture.

Assuming that the myth has a double structure allows us to see Part II as some kind of dramatization of Part I. But if these are indeed two halves, what happens to the young woman in Part II; Why does she seem to disappear? I suggest that she does not: She is the victim of cultural rape in both parts. In Part I, she is the demure prepubescent who should be protected by a chief and, instead, is simply invaded and taken over (colonized, if you will) by him; in Part II, her role is played by the villages and their inhabitants, who—similarly— should have been looked after by their chief and, instead, are invaded and destroyed by him.

In this powerful myth, women's constant and patient nurturing is the standard against which men's selfish adventures are measured (in high contrast to most of the hero stories in Western cultures). The Sun, whose myth it is, prevails; the chief, whose misadventure it is, fails and must start over, poor and alone (one of the most frightening scenarios in family-based tribes). Rather than achieving insight and a boon for his culture (as we would expect if we accepted Joseph Campbell's archetype for the hero), our chief's selfishness impoverishes him and kills his culture. This much, at least, we can see in the story—even without knowing anything about linguistic features (How many images in the story are cultural puns? How many are familiar metaphors?), or about performance styles (Which passages were delivered rapidly or loudly? Where did the narrator pause and for how long? Was the narrator visibly or audibly moved by some part of the performance? Did the narrator tell the story well, or is this version just a tattered remnant of an older, even more magnificent portrait of human selfishness?), or even provenience (Was this a well-known story? Are there similar or parallel stories that comment on chiefs and their behavior, marriageability, gender, individual impulses that might enlarge our sense of what this story means?). Indeed, this story contains some psychological insights that may seem quite modern or sophisticated to us: the recognition that unwillingness to get up may be a symptom of depression, or the tactic of denial or displacement in the chief's insistence that the coveted shining object itself, and not his craving of it, causes his troubles. Are there other insights in the story that are not so obvious?

As superficial as our understanding of the story is, it still emerges as a world classic, in my opinion, partly because of the eloquent and moving way it dramatizes a recognizable human dilemma and partly because the subject is universal and tenaciously contemporary: Someone's reckless and singleminded addiction to a bright object he can't let go of is a topic that is just as gripping today as it has ever been. Dell Hymes said that when he was working on the first full translation of "The Sun's Myth," he could not help but think of his own culture's almost total addiction to the brilliance and power of atomic energy—especially as manifested in the destructive atom bomb (an issue taken up eloquently in Stanley Kubrick's film *Doctor Strangelove*).

But why did Charles Cultee choose to tell this story to Franz Boas in 1891? No doubt we will never know, but it is instructive to contemplate the question, for Native people don't recite myths just for the fun of it. Consider the context for Natives in the Northwest at the turn of the last century: They had been displaced, decimated, exploited, even gunned down. They themselves still tell stories and jokes about how stupid they felt in their first meetings with European goods and technology, which killed them even as they were fascinated by the novelty. Anecdotes like these (illustrated in greater detail in Chapter 7 of *The Anguish of Snails*), plus the strong admonition in stories like "The Sun's Myth" that people make their own moral choices and face the results, allow us to speculate that Charles Cultee saw his own people destroying themselves and their culture in a selfish rush to obtain the bright objects brought by the whites.

Consider the irony in this: One of the last three speakers of the myth's language narrates an old story of cultural disintegration (up until that moment a theoretical construct to be avoided, in large part by adhering to the values in the story) to a visiting white man who can't understand the language (Cultee later translated it phrase by phrase for Boas, using Chinook Jargon, which both of them knew). And consider the immediate scene: A powerful man arrives, presents himself to a powerless Native American who possesses immense narrative riches, and says, in effect, "Whose are these wonderful stories?"—then finally concludes, "I will take them." Did Cultee suddenly see himself unwittingly playing the role of the girl in the story, the innocent local on the verge of losing everything? The fact that Boas was a German Jew, whose people unknowingly stood only a few years away from their own annihilation by a culture they felt themselves an integral part of, makes the irony even deeper for us, if not for Cultee—though I suspect Cultee would not have been surprised.

"The Sun's Myth" is available because a dedicated anthropological folklorist and linguist, Dell Hymes, dedicated a good part of his life to resuscitating a dry, written text collected at Shoalwater, Washington, by a long dead anthropologist and stored away in a dusty volume of Bureau of American Ethnology (BAE) reports. Using his knowledge of the extant Chinookan languages, he was able not only to translate the piece more thoroughly than Boas but also notice stylistic devices that highlighted certain actions and themes and even performance styles that brought scenes into sharp focus. But what about the rest of us who do not have a mastery of Native languages? Where can we go to discover even a part of the majestic Native literary heritage that was being shared with researchers a hundred years ago even as much of it was dying out? The BAE reports are full of wonderful texts, but they are not easy reading. They usually feature a transcription of someone telling a story (set down in a phonetic system that few can read today), followed by a phrase-by-phrase translation of the performed text (in syntax that makes it sound incredibly primitive), accompanied by a prose summary so dry it makes you wonder why anybody bothered.

Take a close look at one of these texts, though, and—even without linguistic training—you notice some connecting or transition words (then, again) repeated in regular positions at the beginning of parallel phrases.

Take these phrases as signs of a delivery style (parallels, repetitions) and write down each of them on a new line, and you have a text that *begins* to look like "The Sun's Myth." You then see that sets of these phrases seem to fit together thematically or rhetorically, like paragraphs. But paragraphs are ways of marking closely associated ideas in writing, and we're not dealing with writing but oral delivery. We don't speak in paragraphs; we speak in aurally recognizable phrases. Thus, it's not as if we are trying to create poetry, per se, but what we perceive is that oral texts, like most poems, are addressed to the ear and not the eye. Forget about all those printers' conventions and think instead of the way someone might recite a long, complex narrative using a style that everyone in the home culture can recognize and understand. The result is a provisional rendering that is a lot more interesting than the ones provided by the early BAE texts. There are phrases you won't understand and others that can be interpreted in two or three different ways in English idiom. Remember that you are not pretending to translate a language you don't know but trying to suck a few drops of juice from a dry lemon: if you get any taste at all, it's more than you had before.

I followed this procedure with the members of a recent seminar on Native American traditional narrative, working through Boas's transcription of a Tsimshian story called "The Grizzly Bear." We had been discussing the great number of stories in various Northwest tribes' traditions where young women inadvertently step in bear droppings (apparently a taboo) and are subsequently carried off (or seduced) by a handsome man who later turns out to be a bear. The woman lives with the bear as his wife in every respect, bearing his children and keeping his household, until, inevitably, hunters from her village (sometimes her own brothers) discover the bear and kill him. These are fascinating stories of intimate interactions and unavoidable frictions between humans and animals, and they are well worth reading and discussing. The Tsimshian story, in contrast, features a man who marries a female grizzly, so we decided it would be interesting to probe the story as far as our limitations allow us.

The following text is my best attempt to offer a composite version of the suggestions made by the members of my class.[5]

The Grizzly Bear
[told by Moses]

[Part 1]
Four men:

> *One the eldest,*
> *then the next eldest,*
> *then also the youngest;*
> *then one great chief, their father.*
> *Then their mother, the wife of the chief.*
> > *Their town was large.*

Well!
By the middle of winter,
everyone's food was gone.
Then, what could they eat?
One [of the brothers] was a hunter,
> *And so was the youngest one.*
Then they remembered what they used to do
> *when there was no food.*
Then they went, the two hunters,

> as well as the eldest, a great man.
Then they went in company.
The eldest one's wife did not go with him;
> only [one of] his brothers went with him.
And they went,
> a long way they went.
Then they found a house,
> and they stayed in it.
In the morning,
> the youngest one rose.
Two were his dogs,
> very powerful dogs.
Then he went.
He carried a spear;
> a blade was on it.
Then he put on snowshoes,
> and he went.
Then he reached the foot of a mountain,
> and he went up.
When he got halfway up,
> he heard his dog's voice above him,
> but he couldn't get to it.
> The mountain was icy.
Then he took a little stone ax,
> and crossways he chopped the ice of the mountain.
Then he reached the tail of a ridge
> where a tree was down.
That's where the dogs were making noise.
> And he reached them.
Look! In the ground was a great grizzly bear,
> two cubs, very large.
Then the man moved toward the hole;
Then she stretched way out and took the man.
Then the cubs took him,
> and they killed him.
Dead the man;
> then his brothers lost him.

When he had been lost about two days,
>*then the next brother rose.*
>*He also had two dogs.*

In the morning, he also went
>*with his two dogs.*

He, too, carried a spear with a blade on it.
Then he, too, went.
When he also found what his brother had found,
>*the dogs also ran upwards.*

Once more also he discovered what his brother had found.
He saw where the ice of the mountain was chipped crossways.
Then he, too, got toward [the hole].
Not long he did so:
>*She took him in, too.*
>*Then the cubs killed him, too.*

Then he, too, was dead,
>*and his two dogs.*

So again a younger brother was lost.
When only one [brother] was left over
>*(a very big improper man),*
>*then he, too, rose.*

Then he, too, went in the morning,
>*also with two dogs;*
>*he also carried a spear.*
>*A blade was on it.*

Then he put on snowshoes.
Then he, too, went on the mountain.
On the same path he went that his brothers had traveled.
Then he heard where the dogs barked.
Then he too reached [the spot].
Then just as he began to place himself,
>*suddenly the great grizzly bear stretched out her paws.*

The great man fell in headfirst.
Then this way he slapped it.
He got his hand right in the great vulva of the great grizzly bear.
Then said the great grizzly bear to her cubs,
>*"My dears! Build up the fire;*

he begins to feel cold, your father."
Very embarrassed was the heart of the great grizzly bear
    because the man felt inside her vulva.
Therefore, it was very good for the man:
    She didn't kill him because he had felt inside [her].
Therefore, she liked him.
Then said the great grizzly bear,
    "I will marry you."
And the great man agreed.
The great woman grizzly bear was glad in her heart
    because the big Indian man married her.
Then always they lay down.

[Part 2]

When he had done so many years,
    He was lost, the great man.
Then said the big man [that he was]
    lonesome for his father,
    and his mother,
    and his wife,
    and his little boy,
    and his little sister.
Then he said he would go out of the woods.
And the great grizzly bear agreed.
"I shall accompany you,"
    she said to the big man.
Then, when it was morning,
    then they went out of the woods.
And they traveled from there to the town.
Then the big man entered.
Then cried the great chief, his great father,
    and his mother,
    and his wife.
Then he entered and sat down.
Then he told [them] that his wife was standing outside.
Then his little sister went out to call his wife,

And she looked around for her outside.
Indeed, the little girl found where the great grizzly bear stood [and]
    fled inside shouting and crying and screaming
    very much afraid:
    "Great ugly thing!
    hohohoho!
    great monster!"
Then the man himself went out,
    the great grizzly bear's own husband.
    And he spoke [to her and] invited her inside.
Then she entered,
    and the great grizzly bear sat down
    where a mat was spread.
That large her paws.
The chief and his wife were very scared.
Then they ate salmon.
    Then the great grizzly bear ate some.
Then [they] put crab apple and grease in a dish,
    and it lay there.
Then the great grizzly bear ate it, too.
The town was very astonished at what he [the man] had done.
Later on, the great grizzly bear said to her husband,
    "Âdo, get your child,"
    she said to her husband.
    "I want to see it."
Then one man went to get the little child.
    And he made the child come;
    then the great grizzly bear wanted [to hold] it.
Then they gave it [to her],
    and the child did not cry.
Then the great grizzly bear said again one day,
    "It would be good if you would invite your wife."
Then the woman came,
    formerly the wife of the man.
    Then she entered
    and sat down near the man, her own husband.
    He [had] newly married the great grizzly bear.

One grizzly bear the wife of the man,
one also a woman of his own town.
The woman had one child,
and the great grizzly bear had none.
[But] there were her children in her house on the mountain;
They hadn't come with her out of the woods.
Well!
They lived this way for many months.
Then, when it came to be summer,
 then, before the berries were ripe,
 then said the great grizzly bear to the woman:
 "Perhaps [the berries] are ripe where I lived."
Then she asked her to go along,
 and they went.
Then they reached there,
 and a few berries were ripe.
Then they picked them:
 The woman put what she picked into her bag, [but] the great
 grizzly did not use a bag;
  her stomach was her bag.
 She ate what she picked.
Then they returned;
 they came from there to the house of their husband.
Then they entered.
Then said the great grizzly bear,
 "It would be good for you to invite the people,"
 she said to the man.
Then one man left who invited many men.
Then the woman took her bag to the middle
 of the house, where the great grizzly bear also was.
Then she said to her husband,
 "Put some dishes back from the fire,"
 and he put some back from the fire.
Then her anus became large,
 and out went the berries she had eaten.
 She said that she had picked them.
 What she ate, she put in [the dishes].

It came out her anus.
Then the dish was full of the berries she prepared.
Then the Indians saw it;
perhaps excrements were in it.
Well!
Then she ordered [someone to take] a dish full of the berries that came out her anus,
and she laid it before the people.
They were afraid to eat it
because perhaps excrements were in it,
because they saw where it had come out her anus.
They ate only the berries prepared by the Indian woman.
The rest they took home
that the great grizzly bear had given them.
Their wives ate it at their own houses.
Well!
Then the great grizzly bear was in good heart.
Well!
When the salmon swam in the water in front of the town,
then the chief made a weir,
and there was a trap;
and there was still another kind of trap.
Then it was finished;
they finished it,
and it was evening.
Then the people lay down.
Just before daylight,
then rose the great grizzly bear.
Then down she went to the weir,
and she saw where the trap was full of salmon,
and she emptied it completely.
Then she took them up inside the house,
and she ordered the chief, the great father-in-law,
to distribute them to the town.
So they distributed them.
Then again it was evening.
Again she did so,

[but] the people didn't know it.
When she had done so for many days,
    she and her cowife had dried many [salmon]
    so that the house was full of what the great grizzly bear and
    her cowife had dried.
Then it was morning,
    and down [to the weir] went one young man.
His heart stood still because he found no salmon.
He saw no salmon at the trap
    since the great grizzly bear had finished them
    and taken them to the house of her husband,
    therefore, he was sick in his heart [angry?].
Then he scolded.
The young man scolded the great grizzly bear.
He was sick in his heart because he did not get anything.
The young man said,
    "You wouldn't quit rising early, great drop-jaw";
    that's what he said to the great grizzly bear.
    He was scolding—that's why he said that.
Twice he scolded [her]:
    "Big Giving-Excrements-for-Food!" he said
    when he again scolded.
Then she took notice of it, the great grizzly bear.
Then she came,
    being sick in her heart.
Then she ran out [of the house],
    greatly angry,
    and she went to where the man was who scolded.
Then she stood in there [in the weir?],
    and she took the man,
    and she killed him all over.
The man was dead,
    his flesh was totally finished.
    All his bones were broken.
At once she left.
She remembered her people,
    where her two cubs were.

Then the great grizzly bear left,
    angry and sick in heart.
Then her husband followed her.
The great grizzly bear said:
    "Âdo! Turn back!
    I might kill you!"
But the man refused
    because he loved his great grizzly bear wife.
A second time the great grizzly bear spoke,
    sent back her husband.
And the husband refused;
    therefore, she did so:
        The great grizzly bear rushed back.
Then she killed him.
Then the man was dead, her own husband.
Then the great grizzly bear left.
The man was dead.

I have an idea that the full meaning and emotional force of this occasionally humorous tragedy will elude us. Even so, many fascinating things are going on in the story, and we can ask some fairly pointed questions about them. For example, we notice several places where the narrator must have illustrated his story with hand gestures, such as when the man "slapped this way" when he accidentally struck the grizzly's vulva by thrashing around, or when the narrator describes the grizzly's hands as "that large her paws." What other gestures, volume levels, facial expressions, or eye contact did he use? We have little indication, for Boas was mostly looking for language examples, not performance styles, unfortunately.

We can observe that the activities in Part I essentially depict male hunters going after meat, while those in Part II describe women harvesting berries and salmon. Part I is mostly about human behavior; Part II is mostly about the behavior of the bear. Part I takes the human characters away from the familiarity of a tribal town and toward unforeseeable, open nature in the woods; Part II takes a bear in the opposite direction: away from the woods and into town. The oldest, "improper" brother is welcomed into the family of the great grizzly bear (once the possibility of killing is converted by the female to sex) in Part I, while the great grizzly is welcomed into the family life of the town (once they get used to her odd way of carrying berries) in Part II. Yet, as we see toward the end, the berries episode is not fully accepted by the people, for the angry young man uses it to scold the bear. And even though the great grizzly works hard to harvest enough salmon to distribute to everyone, she is apparently doing it wrong—presumably by not letting anyone else help in a process that is normally shared among the townspeople. The man, who in Part I has saved his own life by accepting marriage with the grizzly bear (what options did he have, one wonders?), nonetheless eventually misses his family and wants to return to them. In spite of sexual intimacy, life among the bears isn't entirely satisfying; indeed, he is described as "lost." Similarly, though the grizzly in Part II gets along amazingly well with her husband's family and her cowife, calms the baby, supplies food (if you don't mind her processing method), and labors diligently at the fish trap, she somehow isn't fitting in. She is still a grizzly bear living away from her natural element in a human town. When the young sister first sees the grizzly and runs in fear, she is providing an important commentary found in many Northwest stories: The young can often see—and be honest about—something that the grownups are trying to overlook to be polite.

In the stories about women marrying bears, the union lasts a considerable time, and the woman has children by her grizzly husband. Nonetheless, sooner or later, realities seep into the story: Hunters are out looking for bears—that's what hunters do. And eventually they find this bear and kill him (of course, they turn out to be her brothers; that's a kind of economy that focuses any good tale and provides irony). The implication seems to be this: Yes, the bears are our relatives, and yes, you could actually live with one and have children together, but nonetheless they're still bears, and we're still people. We don't act alike; we have different customs. Notice that it is the grizzly bear (not the chief) who tells her husband to summon people to eat berries, and it is she (and not the cooperating members of the tribal community) who gets up early and cleans out the fish trap. She's pushy, perhaps too insistent, unsocialized, and thus—even though she's trying to fit in—still an Other. And she sees it before her husband does: She recognizes the untenable relationship when the angry man at the weir yells at her for getting all the fish and then scolds her for having served them excrements. She realizes she is not at home there and would rather be with her cubs (just as her husband earlier wanted to return to his family). Why doesn't the story simply have her leave in disgust without killing the man? Is it because the vital difference between bears and people could be easily overlooked and romanticized without the tragedy? Is it to show that even bears recognize the gulf between us more readily than do humans blinded by emotion? I wish we knew, but we seem to be standing close to a human classic whose deepest nuances are unfathomable.

That said, it seems to me that the heaviest implication of the story is that, while humans and bears are similar in many respects and considered related, they cannot naturally live together. Perhaps that is why the oldest brother (who—like the oldest sister in the Lummi story—should know better) is called improper. In accepting an unnatural sexual liaison to save his life, in effect trading his personal safety for the food he was supposed to bring back to his starving relatives, he acts improperly. It's as if Part II says to the listeners, "All right, let's play out this same convenient family drama back in the village, where the man normally belongs; let's see how it works in the fabric of tribal society, where the group—not the individual—decides what's normal." And we see that, in spite of the best efforts of the separate actors, the play is a cultural disaster, indeed, a tragedy of sorts in immediate terms. Yet in the long view, normality is restored to the world: The man forfeits his life—as he no doubt would have done had he refused the sexual partnership earlier; the grizzly goes back to her normal world; the town returns to its usual state. This is great stuff, even if we're only catching a small part of its total possibilities.

Our capacity to understand such stories increases immensely when we actually see and hear a performance by a gifted storyteller in the context of his or her own culture. We then can witness the gestural and vocal nuances of the performer and the responses of the audience, and if we're lucky, we can ask questions. I've spent countless long winter evenings listening to stories among Navajo families, everyone sitting around the perimeter of a hogan (or the living room of a house) as one or another adult slowly and quietly narrated a "Coyote story" while a fire snapped in the stove. Each story was followed by a respectful silence, and then someone—often a child—asked for some clarification, and a long conversation developed. Once, when I took a group of reservation high school teachers to such an evening, they came out into the cold night air at about 1:00 a.m. and said, "No wonder these kids are so tired when they get to school in the morning; they've been in a literary seminar all night!"

One evening in the winter of 1955 or '56, while I was living with the Little Wagon family in Montezuma Canyon, we had a visit from a small family which was traveling by wagon down the canyon from Hatch Trading Post. It had started snowing, and the family stopped overnight with us. Late in the evening, one of the children asked where snow came from, and old Little Wagon quietly responded with a story in which his own great grandfather found and returned some sacred fire to the *yei*, the Holy People, who had accidentally dropped it from their fireplace. As a reward to the young man, they dumped their ashes into Montezuma Canyon every year when they cleaned off their hearths and have done so ever since. When the little boy hesitantly asked his father why it also snowed in far-off Blanding, Little Wagon calmly said, "Well, you'll have to make up your *own* story for that." After the visitors left the next morning, the old man remarked that you can tell when children have been to school because they don't have any idea what stories are all about.

Well, what are they about? And how can we learn at least part of the answer by witnessing a live performance? Keeping in mind everything in this chapter thus far, let's take a look at my notation of an actual performance, a story told to his family by my friend Yellowman back in 1956. I had no tape recorder then, so I jotted down the story on scraps of paper as he told it. Fortunately, his delivery was very slow, and I had already heard the story several times. Although the words were not always the same, I had been able to put together a kind of outline, which I filled in with particulars as this performance took place. Here is an account of the live presentation and the responses of the audience.

Ma'i [Coyote] was going along there just as he has always been going along.

[pause of several seconds; the audience is smiling]

Up ahead, near some trees, some junipers, in some junipers, he could see birds flying up.

[slight pause]

They were flying up and looking all around; they could see everywhere.

[pause; the audience is smiling in anticipation]

Ma'i said to them, "Come here, my relatives, give me your eyes so I can see as far as you can."

[longer pause; some children are laughing quietly]

"No, you're not a bird. You can't fly."

[general laughter, including narrator]

Ma'i said to them, "My relatives, please give me your eyes. Take mine out and give me yours."

[pause; smiling]

"No [emphatically]! You're not a bird!"

[pause; smiling]

Ma'i said, "My relatives, I want to see like you; please take my eyes out and put yours in!"

[pause, deep breath]

"No! You're not a bird. You can't fly!"

[pause; some laughter]

Ma'i said, "My relatives, please take my eyes out and give me yours!"

[pause; smiling]

"Yaahdilah! [no translation; an expletive]"

[general prolonged laughter]

They came to him. They took sticks and pried out his eyes.

[loud laughter]

"Aah!" he was screaming. He cried. "That hurts!"

[louder laughter, including narrator]

They pried out his eyes.

[mild laughter]

They flew away.

[smiling, nodding heads]

He was blind. He couldn't see anything.
> [pause; smiles]

He stumbled around in the junipers, feeling his way.
> [pause]

He was crying.
> [pause]

Ma'i felt some lumps on the side of the juniper, that pitch that grows there.
> [pause; someone says, "Hmm."]

He felt those lumps, and he pulled them off the tree: Two lumps of pitch, the same size as his eyes, perhaps.
> [short pause]

He put them into his sockets.
> [pause; several people expel air through their noses]

Now Ma'i has yellow eyes; his eyes are pitch.
> [long pause, several seconds]

That's what they say.

By now, I am sure you recognize that the main point of the story is not explaining how coyotes got yellow eyes; indeed, you're probably guessing (correctly) that, like the Lummi story, this one acts as a reminder: When we see a coyote, we note that he has yellow eyes and remember this story. So where's the action in the story? What is being dramatized? Coyote wants to be able to see from above ground, like the birds, and is unwilling to accept their admonition that his desire is not appropriate. Coyotes aren't birds. But Coyote insists four times (the key number in most Southwest Native stories), and at that point the birds abandon their advice and say "*yaahdilah!*"— the equivalent of "all right, dammit, *you* take the responsibility!" And his insistence on seeing what is not normal for him is turned into pain and blindness—a much more powerful form of instruction than the simple advice, "Children, don't overstep your bounds in nature, or it may be painful."

But what do we learn from the dynamics of the live performance? For one thing, we see that the Navajo narrator (in this case, Yellowman) pauses considerably between lines or phrases in a way that may make the telling a bit slow for people who are accustomed to reading or hearing stories delivered with greater verve and urgency. What accounts for this? Among many reasons, the Navajo narrator wants the images in each phrase to sink in, but more importantly, many Native speaking customs incorporate silence as a preparation for saying something important. If someone in a group is quiet for a noticeable time, it may mean that the person is about to say something especially noteworthy. In addition, many Native speakers and narrators repeat a key idea four times (the same practice often occurs in ritual songs, where the four-way repetition may remind us of the directions and thus surroundment). Interestingly enough, many Natives report that in conversation they are always interrupted by non-Natives, who don't understand the rhythm in this kind of foregrounding. The fourfold repetition in this story appears in the scene where Ma'i begs the birds for their eyes, and in each case is refused until step four, when he reaches the limits of making his demand, and the birds feel obliged to teach him a lesson. You can tell from the responses of the audience that they know what's coming: They have not only heard the story before but are also familiar with the structural convention. But they are also laughing, so we need to consider what's so funny about prying out a coyote's eyes.

The Navajos often use laughter to comment on children's actions; it's a gentle way of correcting behavior since no one likes to be laughed at. Obviously, people laugh for other reasons as well, especially at jokes or stories where someone does something outlandish: On one hand, it's registering amusement at something odd, and at the same time, it signals that we recognize the discrepancy between the normal and the odd. In the Navajo Ma'i stories, as I've argued elsewhere, laughter seems most pronounced just before or after Ma'i does something that is not only odd but also wrong: He betrays his best friends, he's gluttonous, he's oversexed, he insists on doing things inappropriate for coyotes. In recognizing that these actions are wrong (and they are wrong in *human* behavior; we're not talking about coyote morality), the audience laughs as if to say, "You wouldn't ever see me doing something like that!" And since audience members already know the story and can follow the fourfold structure, they can anticipate where these moments of moral concern surface in the narrative.

In addition, there are probably hundreds of Ma'i stories, some told more often than others, some told more regularly by some storytellers. Most of them are pretty widely known among Navajos and are told in a certain sequence over the course of the winter so that listeners hearing one story can easily remember others with similar motifs. They represent, in today's popular term, "intertextual" entities, although of course the people and the live performances activate the interchange (the idea that texts enjoy some kind of interaction derives from written, not oral, literature). A great number of these stories depict Ma'i trying to do something appropriate for other living beings: He's trying to intrude on nature's norms. In one story, he begs the Lizard People to show him how to slide downhill on flat stones the way they do; they warn him he will be killed, and finally, after his fourth plea, they say "*yaahdilah!*" and show him how to do it, whereupon he promptly kills himself and has to be resuscitated by the Ant People. In another, he begs the Beaver People to let him gamble with them. They are throwing spears through rolling hoops, keeping score. Whoever gets the lowest score has to give up his hide. After his fourth entreaty, he is allowed to play, but of course he loses his hide and has to be buried in the ground for a year while it grows back (his coat is still scraggly today).

Two stories in particular are close in theme to the one already quoted, and the audience's laughter is based in part on its ability to bring the stories together. In one, Ma'i is trying to betray his hunting partner, Skunk (Gólízhii, literally "one with stinking urine") by getting him to take his eyes out so Ma'i can jump him and eat him. Ma'i suggests they play the old game of Throw Our Eyes Up in the Air, but Skunk doesn't know the game and has to be shown. Ma'i takes his eyes out and throws them into the air, saying, "Come back to my sockets!" but they get caught around the branch of a juniper tree (yes, in the same juniper grove as the first story), and Ma'i is blind. He gropes around the tree trunk, finds a couple of pitch balls, and puts them into his sockets. Still not able to see very well (appropriate, of course, since he almost never can "see" where his actions are taking him), he crawls too close to the campfire (where he originally had planned to roast Skunk) and melts the pitch, which runs down into the corners of his eyes (you may have noticed the brown matter in the corners of dogs' and coyotes' eyes).

In the related story, Ma'i is trotting along near a stand of junipers on the edge of a cliff. He sees the birds flying out of the trees and soaring over the canyon and then coming back. He begs them to teach him how to fly, but they point out that they have lightning under their wings, and he has none; moreover, he has no wings. He insists that it has to do with feathers and begs them to give him some. Finally, after the fourth plea, they say "*yaahdilah!*" and each bird pulls a feather out and sticks it to Ma'i's body with a small piece of, yes, juniper pitch. Ma'i launches himself off the cliff and tries to flap his arms but drops straight down to the desert floor to his death.

The story I've included, where Ma'i approaches the birds and begs to use their eyes, brings a whole cluster of Navajo beliefs and stories about Ma'i's selfishness and self-abuse to mind. For one thing, the juniper (*gad*) twists as it grows so it can watch the sun. Its seeds (called *gadbináá'*—literally "juniper's eyes") are used in necklaces and bracelets to remind the wearer of important relationships with nature, which Ma'i insists on breaking. When the birds remind him that he can't fly, they're referring to the story when he unsuccessfully tried flying. When he painfully loses his eyes because of his insistence, the audience can easily react by asking, "Won't he ever learn?" They shake their heads and look briefly at each other as if to say, "There he goes again!"

But even so, as Yellowman told me on several occasions, these stories are not about bad-boy coyotes but rather, about those unmanageable actions of Ma'i which represent human inclinations, foibles, and acts of selfishness which are destructive to us. When I asked Yellowman why these stories differ about the appearance of coyotes' eyes (are they yellow because of the pitch, or are they melted—and thus no longer yellow or even eyes?), he grew quite impatient and gave his favorite explanation for my lack of understanding: The missionaries must have taught me to question Navajo beliefs. Those stories aren't about what coyotes look like, he assured me; they are ways of reminding us about our health. We bring most afflictions upon ourselves by our own actions or inattention to details. Ma'i's dramatizations (my wording, not his) act out a number of important moral issues about inappropriate behavior without actually naming them.

This has a double significance: (1) Navajo language is thought to create reality. Thus, we don't want to talk directly about things which we do not wish to have happen. A doctor telling a man he must take his medicine or he will die sounds to a Navajo as if the doctor is trying to kill his patient. Talking openly about witchcraft strengthens the very practice we do not want to have anything to do with; (2) the structure of the Navajo language contains much of this logic about volition and accountability. In a famous example cited by Gary Witherspoon, you can say, "The man kicked the horse" in Navajo, but you can't say, "The horse kicked the man" because the man is more articulate and intelligent than a horse, and therefore, a horse cannot kick a man. If a man is kicked by a horse, he has brought it on himself by being in the wrong place, handling the animal incorrectly, or just not paying proper attention to what he's doing. Thus, you have to say, "The man got himself kicked by the horse." The same logic applies to human health: If you are sick, it's not an accident that happened to you; in some way, you got yourself in the way of it or brought it on, or perhaps someone inflicted it on you intentionally.[6] One way to encourage people—especially children, who don't consciously recognize all this yet—to protect themselves is to remind them not to mistreat their bodies, not to step outside the natural relationships in nature, not to betray friends and relatives, not to be selfish with resources. Rather than talk about these behaviors openly, which may have the effect of encouraging them, the traditional Navajo presents them through the dramatizations of that amorphous figure, Ma'i, ostensibly a coyote but really less *a* coyote than the epitome of coyoteness.

Of course, similar characters fill the stories of many tribes, especially from the Plains westward. Among the Sioux, it is Inktomi or Oktomi, who is depicted as a spider. In some tribes, he is a rabbit (as far as I know, he is always masculine, which probably reflects the tribal notion that aberrant behavior is most likely to be male). In the far Northwest, he is Raven. Though non-Natives have dubbed him Trickster, and some even believe the figure is a universal archetype, in fact you'll notice (if you encounter enough stories) that the American Indian Coyote character seldom tricks anyone the way that Anansi, the African trickster, does. Rather, he's mostly depicted as underfed, oversexed, unprincipled in selfishness, vengeful—in other words, the epitome of everything we should not be; and at the same time, he is a sacred creator who changes the nature of the world as he goes—the epitome of what we are not in a position to do. In this latter role, we find among the Northwest tribes accounts of Old Man Coyote creating the geographical world (to be sure, sometimes by depositing his turds, which can still be seen), teaching humans how to copulate (to be sure, by playing the active role himself), deciding which rivers will have salmon and which ones won't (to be sure, based on which chiefs send their most luscious daughters downstream to him), and even explaining minute human details like the white stuff in the corners of our eyes in the morning (he wipes his penis in his grandchildren's eyes so they won't notice he has been in bed with their mother, his daughter-in-law).

What virtually all these stories have in common is a strong, often unforgettable, central image, which reminds us again and again of the moral point of the drama. A pile of rocks on the Oregon coast marks the place where Coyote suffered from diarrhea caused by a small plant he ate in anger; the plant—used (sparingly) for constipation—can still be found there. The white stuff we clean out of our eyes every morning reminds us not to commit incest and also not to judge others before we can see clearly. A juniper grove may remind us to live within nature's system rather than challenge it. A far-off glimpse of a coyote with yellow eyes makes us remember not to abuse our body parts (or simply not make light of everything, as living coyotes seem to do).

A story told especially to teenagers by many tribes on the Northwest coast and along the Columbia River describes Coyote sitting on one shore of the river, lusting after a group of five women who are bathing on the other side. Not wanting to get cold and wet, he commands his penis to grow across the river and enter the women one by one. In one version of the story, the girls think they are being attacked by a water monster and immediately cut its head off with an obsidian knife. In another, he succeeds in copulating with the women, but as he tries to pull his penis back across the river, the sturgeon and other fish attack it and tear it to shreds. By the time he gets it back, it's all in tatters and can't be used. And of course, he almost immediately meets a pretty coyote woman who invites him home, an invitation he must decline because he can't function normally. Can you think of a more powerful image to drive home the idea that ignoring custom and misusing your sexual organs are self-destructive actions that prevent you from leading a normal life? Yet the narrative doesn't make this statement overtly; it embeds the concepts in a mental drama which depends on the audience for its realization.[7]

A similar impression is created by tribal songs, even though they are usually far from narrative in their presentation. To put it most simply, what the narratives accomplish by dramatic patterning of cultural values the songs accomplish by musical and verbal nuance. Patterning is there, usually in the stanza format and four-way or five-way repetition of lines or phrases, but the weight is carried even more by recollections and associations in the listeners' minds, and the impact of most of these is difficult (unlike the narratives) to demonstrate in print. For example, a song made up entirely of *vocables*, syllables with no lexical meaning, may bring tears to the eyes of someone who remembers an aged relative singing it long ago, even though on the page it doesn't seem very provocative:

> *Hey-ey-ey-ey ha-ney ha-ney ya-a-a-a,*
> *hey-ey-ey-ey ha-ney ha-ney ya-a-a-a.*

If you attend a powwow, you'll hear many songs like this; each, however, has a different tune and is so unique in its sequence of verses that dancers can anticipate the end and stop dancing exactly with the last beat.

One Navajo song, often heard when a ritual stick is transported from one location to another during a sequence of ceremonies, has no words but is all meaning:

> *Hey yanga hey yo, hey yo hey yanga.*
> *hey yanga hey yo, hey yo hey yanga.*
> *Hey yo hey ya, hey yo hey yo hey,*
> *ya hey yo hey yo hey yanga.*

Repeated four times, the song is normally sung on horseback, so almost every syllable has two beats to it (like *hey-ey ya-anga-a hey-ey yo-oo-hey yo-o hey-ey ya-anga-a*). Any Navajo who has heard it in its normal context immediately thinks of fifty to one hundred men on horseback, late at night, in the winter, singing this song in a high tenor voice together as they pass by on the way to where tomorrow's session of the ceremony will be held. Now, that's evocative. But the context is so musical that it is better illustrated by actually hearing the song live or on recordings, so I will focus on a few examples where words project culturally shared nuance.

At a powwow, you may hear this recent war-dance song:[8]

> *Mickey Mouse, Minnie Mouse, Pluto, too:*
> They all live in Disneyland,
> *Hey ya, hey ya, hey ya yo;*
> Mickey Mouse, Minnie Mouse, Pluto, too:
> They all work at Disneyland,
> *Hey ya, hey ya, hey ya yo!*

Or intelligible lines surfacing in a song otherwise made up of vocables:

> *Oh yes, I love you honey,*
> *eeya han nigh yo*
> I don't care if you married sixteen times;
> I'll get you yet,
> *Hey ya, na eya han nigh yo.*

Sometimes at singing parties known as "forty-nines," you can hear very brief humorous verses:

> *Shame on you,*
> *Shame on you, girl,*
> *your knees are floating along below your dress.*

Apparently, this is a comment on minidresses. Or here's one from the 1930s, sung in English, "Wait for me, darlin'; after the dance is over, I'm coming to get you in my one-eyed Ford."

More serious are the songs which, in elliptical fashion, capture a process in nature. Judith Vander provides a number of striking examples in the Naraya (Ghost Dance) songs sung by several Shoshone women. One of them translates phrase by phrase into English as follows:

> *Eagle's wing is skying,*
> *Eagle's wing is skying.*
> *Green water shiny under lying while moving,*
> *Green water shiny under lying while moving.*

The singer, Emily Hill, comments, "That eagle's flying, his wings way up there in the sky, looking down to earth and seeing the water shining and the grass on the earth green." Vander rightly uses the term "haikulike" for songs like this.[9]

As provocative are the Deer Songs of the Yaqui, who live in the Sonoran Desert near Tucson, Arizona. The Yaqui sing of the *sea ania*, the flower world which is thought to embody perfectly all the beauty of the natural world, complete with all its plants, animals, birds, insects, and water. On ritual occasions when the spirit of the deer is invoked (in part by a dancer who wears a small deer's head on top of his own), the songs describe the perfect deer moving through the Utopian *sea ania* and being hunted—phrased from the deer's point of view. In the morning, the deer sings,

> *You are an enchanted flower wilderness world,*
> *You are an enchanted wilderness world,*
> *you lie with see-through freshness.*
> *You are an enchanted flower wilderness world,*
> *you are an enchanted wilderness world,*
> *you lie with see-through freshness.*

Later, while being hunted, the deer sings,

> *Not wanting to die,*
> *dodging through the wilderness.*
> *Not wanting to die,*
> *dodging through the wilderness.*

And later,

> *Over there, I, in an opening*
>> *in the flower-covered grove,*
>>> *as I am walking,*
>> *alongside*
>>> *the flower-covered grove,*
>>>> *as I am walking,*
>> *with my head hanging down*
>>> *toward the ground,*
>>>> *as I am walking,*
>> *with foam*
>>> *around my mouth,*
>>>> *as I am walking,*
> *Exhausted from running, you are walking;*
>> *exhausted from running, you are moving.*

And finally, after he has been killed, the deer finds himself upside down, being carried back on a pole by the hunters:

> *Over there, I, in an opening*
>> *in the flower-covered grove,*
>>> *as I am walking,*
> *Just I, flower person's wooden bow*
>> *has taken me.*
> *Flower person's flower bamboo arrow*
>> *has overpowered me in an enchanted way.*
> *What happened to me that my hands*
>> *are over my antler crown?*

Such a song allows listeners to think of nature and vicariously experience it from the perspectives of the animals and plants which animate the world.[10] For the singers, of course, giving voice to the words and music becomes an even more personal experience requiring concentration, breath, muscle, voice, commitment. For the Deer Dancer and others involved in the ceremonies, the experience becomes even deeper through the intensified use of the body and its gestures.

None of this has to do with explaining anything about deer or nature or commenting philosophically about ecology. This is a process which uses words and tones to touch off shared values among closely associated people: It is a culturally structured way of thinking and experiencing together the patterns which make us real. As Yellowman insisted, "We need a strong way of thinking about things; stories make things possible. Without stories and songs, nothing would be possible, nothing would exist."

NOTES

1. Paul Zolbrod, Diné bahane' *The Navajo Creation Story* (Albuquerque: University of New Mexico Press, 1984). His "Altsé Hástiin" appears in Brian Swann, ed., *Coming to Light: Contemporary Translations of the Native American Literatures of North America* (New York: Random House, 1994), 614–23. Sam D. Gill, *Sacred Words: A Study of Navajo Religion and Prayer* (Westport, Conn.: Greenwood Press, 1981) discusses the active, hortatory ways in which Navajo ritual speech is thought to bring about real change in the human condition. Gladys A. Reichard, *Navaho Religion: A Study of Symbolism* (Princeton: Princeton University Press, 1974) provided the first thorough discussion of Navajo narrative ritual acts. Leland C. Wyman, *Blessingway* (Tucson: University of Arizona Press, 1970) offers an analytical and comparative study of three different versions of the basic "main stem" of the Navajo ritual system.

2. The assertion that the capacity for story is uniquely expressive of human behavior and thinking was put forward by Professor Renee Fuller at a meeting of the American Psychological Association in the 1970s and reported to the general reader in *Brain and Mind: Frontiers of Research, Theory, and Practice* 5, no. 2 (December 1979): 1–2. John Niles's brilliant *Homo Narrans: The Poetics and Anthropology of Oral Literature* (Philadelphia: University of Pennsylvania Press, 1999) deals mainly with the northern European heritage of oral narratives, but many of its assertions relate to what we discuss here. A collection of essays edited by Joseph F. Trimmer, *Narration as Knowledge* (Portsmouth, N.H.: Boynton/Cook, 1997), explores the application of this concept to the field of teaching in the contemporary world.

3. John Bierhorst's concepts of double myth structure are proposed in his anthology, *The Red Swan: Myths and Tales of the American Indians* (New York: Farrar, Straus and Giroux, 1976), especially pp. 9–10.

4. Dell Hymes's "The Sun's Myth" also appears in Brian Swann, ed., *Coming to Light: Contemporary Translations of the Native American Literatures of North America*, 273–85. His article, "Variation and Narrative Competence," appears in Lauri Honko, ed., *Thick Corpus, Organic Variation and Textuality in Narrative Tradition*, Studia Fennica, Folkloristica 7 (Helsinki: Finnish Literature Society, 2000), 77–92.

5. "The Grizzly Bear" was told by Moses (no other name is provided) to Franz Boas near the mouth of the Nass River in British Columbia in 1894. The text (along with many others like it) is printed in *Tsimshian Texts*, Smithsonian Institution, Bureau of American Ethnology Bulletin 27 (Washington, D.C.: 1902), 200–210. The names of the students in the class who did the translation are as follows: Reed Cornia, Kim Fitzgerald, Steve Hatcher, Dan Haws, Fayth Marrelli, Eric Nankervis, Robin A. Parent, Krystel Poulsen, Paulette Roberts, Trevor Smith, Michael Spooner, Wynne Summers, Tomoyo Tamayama, Donna Vance, Harriet White, and Nora Zambreno.

6. Gary Witherspoon's amazing study of the Navajo language is *Art and Language in the Navajo Universe* (Ann Arbor: University of Michigan Press, 1977). In it, among other things, we learn that the Navajo verb system has 356,200 distinct conjugations for the verb "to go" (p. 21) and that "in the Navajo view of the world, language is not a mirror of reality; reality is a mirror of language" (p. 34).

7. For information on Coyote and Coyote stories, see William Bright, *A Coyote Reader* (Berkeley: University of California Press, 1993). The term "trickster" is not really descriptive of the complex character (who seldom tricks anyone).

8. For the "Mickey Mouse" song, I am indebted to Craig Miller of the Folk Arts Program at the Utah Arts Council, who recorded it at a powwow in southern Utah.

9. More Ghost Dance songs, as well as powwow and social songs, can be found in Judith Vander's rich and sensitive study, *Songprints: The Musical Experience of Five Shoshone Women* (Urbana: University of Illinois Press, 1988). The concept of musical *experience*, not just recitation, is germane to our discussion. The eagle Naraya song and the singer's comment on it appear on page 19.

10. The Yaqui songs are published in Larry Evers and Felipe S. Molina, eds., *Yaqui Deer Songs / Maso Bwikam: A Native American Poetry* (Tucson: University of Arizona Press, 1987). The songs quoted partially here can be found in their complete form on pp. 104, 164, 165, and 167. The Yaqui evocation of a lush, dewy "flower world" as the epitome of their Sonoran desert environment is one of the most striking examples of the triumph of poetry and song over everyday reality.

About the Author

Barre Toelken, longtime director of the Utah State University Folklore Program (1985–2003), is the author or editor of numerous books and articles on folklore and related topics. Among these are *The Dynamics of Folklore*; *Morning Dew and Roses: Nuance, Metaphor, and Meaning in Folksongs*; *Ghosts and the Japanese* (with Michiko Iwasaka); *Native American Oral Traditions: Collaboration and Interpretation* (with Larry Evers); and *The Anguish of Snails: Native American Folklore in the West*, winner of the Chicago Folklore Prize. In 2011, Toelken was awarded the Kenneth Goldstein Award for Lifetime Academic Leadership, by the American Folklore Society.

Toelken remains suspicious of any theory that is conceptualized as the way that "all folklore works." Such ideological frameworks may leave important aspects of cultures completely out of consideration. Folklorists, according to Toelken, may be blinded by what they *want* to see, rather than awakened by what is *really there*. He can say as much only because he admits he learned that painful lesson personally. Moreover, folklorists miss the boat when they select or mold lore to fit their theoretical models. Toelken believes that such models are important, but only as a basis for understanding. The center of his work and his thinking is not in the texts but in the people. As he says in *The Dynamics of Folklore*,

> Folklore is dynamic, alive, variant, and persistent. Among folklorists, it might seem absurdly elementary to reiterate, but the *folklore* should come first, the literature second. The meat of our scholarship is in the lore itself, not in the theory. From the Arctic to Tierra del Fuego, culture and worldview change with each tribe, and literary people are tragically missing out, often choosing not to deal with the dizzying array of cultural performance and meaning, so they work with theoretical models instead of people. The more sad for them.

About the Book

AMONG MANY STUDIES HE PRODUCED over a distinguished career as an academic folklorist, Barre Toelken's richest and perhaps his most personal work is *The Anguish of Snails: Native American Folklore in the West*. Within a framework of performance theory, cultural worldview, and collaborative research, he examines Native American visual arts, dance, oral tradition (story and song), humor, and patterns of thinking and discovery. In the process he considers popular distortions of native beliefs, demystifies many traditions by showing how they can be comprehended within their cultural contexts, considers why some aspects of Native American life are not meant to be understood by or shared with outsiders, and emphasizes how much can be learned through sensitivity to and awareness of cultural values.

Winner of the 2004 Chicago Folklore Prize, *The Anguish of Snails* is an essential work for the collection of any serious reader in folklore or Native American studies.

Current Arguments in Folklore

Uᴛᴀʜ Sᴛᴀᴛᴇ Uɴɪᴠᴇʀsɪᴛʏ Pʀᴇss's Cᴜʀʀᴇɴᴛ Arguments in Folklore is a series of short-form publications of provocative original material and selections from foundational titles by leading thinkers in the field. Perfect for the folklore classroom as well as the professional collection, this series provides access to important introductory content as well as innovative new work intended to stimulate scholarly conversation. Volumes are available in paperback or ebook form.